My Science Library

Energy All Around

by Buffy Silverman

Science Content Editor:
Shirley Duke

Rourke
Educational Media

rourkeeducationalmedia.com

Teacher Notes available at
rem4teachers.com

Science Content Editor: Shirley Duke holds a bachelor's degree in biology and a master's degree in education from Austin College in Sherman, Texas. She taught science in Texas at all levels for twenty-five years before starting to write for children. Her science books include *You Can't Wear These Genes, Infections, Infestations, and Diseases, Enterprise STEM, Forces and Motion at Work, Environmental Disasters,* and *Gases.* She continues writing science books and also works as a science content editor.

www.rourkeeducationalmedia.com

Photo credits: Cover © alphaspirit; Table of Contents © Yegor Korzh; Page 4 © Yuri Arcurs; Page 5 © (Chart) HitToon.Com, Ovchynnikov Oleksii, Tribalium, Mi.Ti., jupeart, lineartestpilot, Mushakesa, Miguel Angel Salinas Salinas, ohmmy3d, sgame; Page 6 © davidunndderriese, Veyronik; Page 7 © siamionau pavel, ilker canikligil; Page 8 © auremar; Page 9 © Henry Roscoe, Valentyn Volkov; Page 10 © Iakov Kalinin, VVO; Page 11 © Netfalls - Remy Musser, Gringer; Page 12 © deezign; Page 13 © Andrea Danti; Page 12/13 © manfredxy; Page 14 © Arlene Treiber; Page 14 © Yegor Korzh; Page 16/17 © Belinda Pretorius; Page 18 © Kodda; Page 19 © debra hughes, NuConcept, Twinkie Artcat, Neyro, Photo Grafix Black Rhino Illustration; Page 20 © Monkey Business Images; Page 21 © fstockfoto;

Editor: Kelli Hicks

My Science Library series produced by Blue Door Publishing, Florida for Rourke Educational Media.

Library of Congress PCN Data

Silverman, Buffy
 Energy All Around / Buffy Silverman
    p. cm. -- (My Science Library)
 ISBN 978-1-61810-095-5 (Hard cover) (alk. paper)
 ISBN 978-1-61810-228-7 (Soft cover)
 Library of Congress Control Number: 2012930296

Rourke Educational Media
Printed in the United States of America,
North Mankato, Minnesota

Educational Media

rourkeeducationalmedia.com

customerservice@rourkeeducationalmedia.com
PO Box 643328 Vero Beach, Florida 32964

Table of Contents

What is Energy?   4

Heat Energy   10

Motion Energy   14

Fuel Energy   18

Show What You Know   22

Glossary   23

Index   24

What is Energy?

Think of the energy used to make your breakfast. A chicken used energy from its food to make eggs. Then the chicken laid the eggs. The eggs were stored in a refrigerator that uses **electricity** to stay cool. You turned on a stove that used energy to make heat to cook the eggs. Your body used energy to mix, chew, and digest the eggs.

Your body uses energy to do everything, including homework!

Sun → Corn → Chicken → Eggs →

Coal → Electricity → Refrigerator → Cooling Eggs

Gas → Stove → Pan → Cooking Eggs

Your Breakfast → You → Digesting Breakfast

stomach

We get energy from many sources, including food and fuel.

What is energy? Scientists define energy as the ability to do work. For example, work occurs when something is moved, or when it is heated or cooled. Plants and animals need energy to grow, move, live, and reproduce.

Plants use the Sun's energy to make food through a process called **photosynthesis**. All other living things depend on plants' ability to turn the Sun's energy into food energy.

Plants use light from the Sun to get energy. Many animals, including humans, eat plants to get energy.

Machines also do work.
Bulldozers use energy
stored in fuel to move.

Many scientists' work led to an understanding that energy cannot be created or destroyed. When we use energy, we change it from one form to another. All forms of energy belong to one of two groups: **potential energy** or **kinetic energy**.

Potential energy is stored energy. Stretch a bow and it has potential energy. Release the bow and it shoots the arrow forward. The bow's potential energy turns into energy of motion, called kinetic energy.

In 1845, James Prescott Joule showed that heat, electrical power, and mechanical power are all forms of energy. He also showed that one form of energy can be changed into another. In 1847, Hermann von Helmholtz proved that when energy changes form, the total amount of energy stays the same.

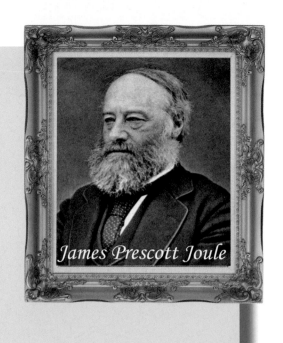

James Prescott Joule

Logs have potential energy stored inside them. Make a campfire and that energy is turned into heat energy.

9

Heat Energy

Visit a beach on a summer day. The Sun's rays heat up the sand. The heat energy in sand moves to your feet and warms them.

The Sun's rays

Heat energy from sand

You run across hot sand and splash into cold water. Now your feet cool down. The heat from your feet moves into the cooler water. Heat energy flows from hot objects to cooler objects.

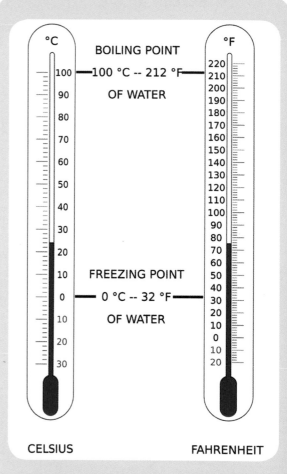

Heat energy from feet flowing to cooler water.

A thermometer measures the temperature of an object. This thermometer shows two different scales. Fahrenheit (F) is the official temperature scale in the United States, and Celsius (C) is the official temperature scale of most other countries.

A **solar** collector uses the Sun's energy to heat water or air. Sun shines on a dark-colored collector. The dark surface absorbs light energy and turns it into heat. Water-filled pipes run through the collector. As the collector heats up, heat moves into the water and warms it. People use the hot water for washing and bathing.

Solar Energy

Energy from the Sun is called solar energy. It is a renewable form of energy, which means that it can be replaced in a short time period.

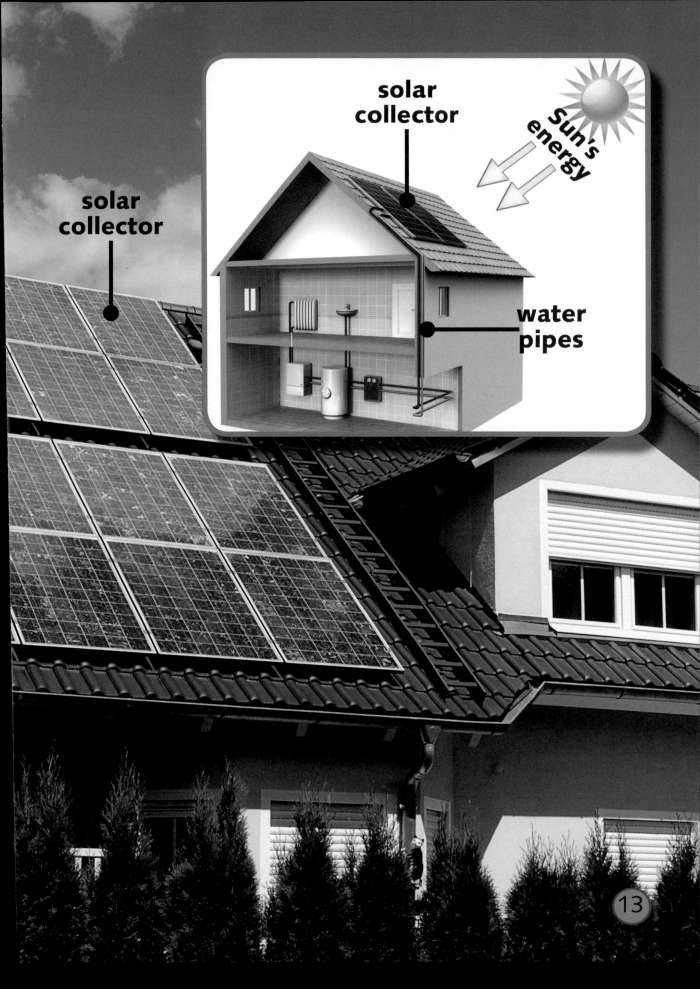

solar
collector

solar
collector

Sun's
energy

water
pipes

Motion Energy

Everything that moves has motion energy. Wind, water, cars, airplanes, and people have motion energy. Imagine finding a rock on top of a hill. The rock has potential energy because of its height and the pull of gravity. You use energy to push the rock and set it in motion. Then the rock tumbles down the hill. If the rock crashes into a fence, it releases its energy all at once. It may knock the fence down!

Before they fell, the loose rocks had potential energy. As they were falling they had motion (kinetic) energy.

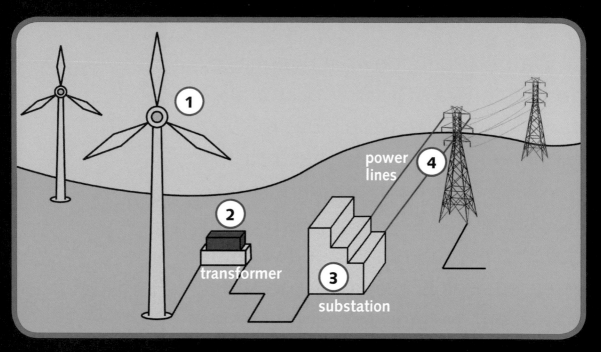

1. Motion energy from wind turns the blades on a wind turbine. The blades turn a shaft, which spins a generator inside the turbine. The generator makes electricity.

2. The electricity travels through a transformer (equipment that changes electrical power from one voltage to a different voltage), to a substation.

3. The substation increases voltage for transmission over long distances.

4. Electricity is transmitted to the grid for our use.

Water rushing down a river has enough energy to carry rocks and carve riverbanks. People use this motion energy to make electricity. A dam at a **hydropower** plant stops a flowing river. Water behind the dam collects in a reservoir. When water is released, it falls over a turbine and spins a magnet inside coiled wires. This motion makes electricity.

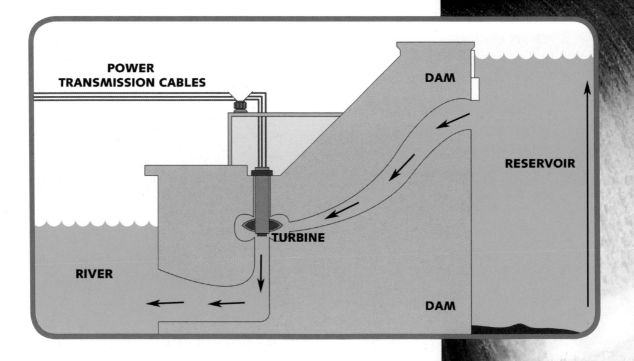

POWER TRANSMISSION CABLES

DAM

RESERVOIR

TURBINE

RIVER

DAM

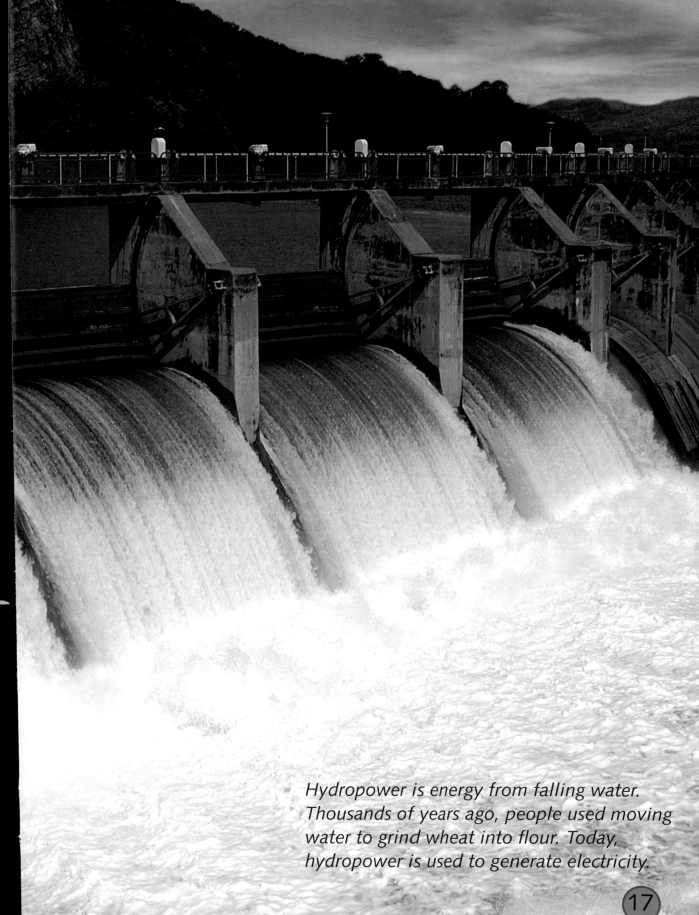

Hydropower is energy from falling water. Thousands of years ago, people used moving water to grind wheat into flour. Today, hydropower is used to generate electricity.

Fuel Energy

Most of the energy we use comes from fuels like petroleum, natural gas, and coal. These fuels are called **fossil fuels**. They formed from the remains of dead plants and animals. After being buried for hundreds of millions of years, the fossils turn into fuel. Chemicals in these fuels store energy.

coal burning power plant

Fossil fuels are called nonrenewable energy because they cannot be replaced in a short time period. When fossil fuels are burned, potential energy from ancient plants and animals is changed into heat energy.

How Coal is Formed

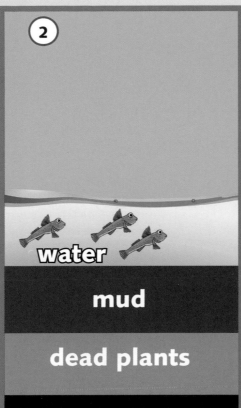

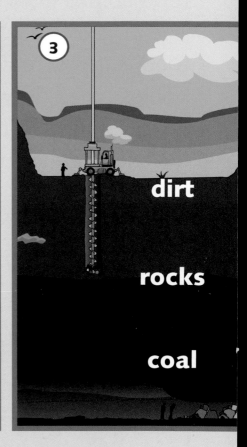

1. 300 million years ago, many plants died in swamps.

2. Over millions of years, the plant remains were buried under water and mud. Ancient oceans dried up or receded.

3. Heat and pressure turned the dead plants into coal.

The food that we eat is also a kind of fuel energy. Like fossil fuels, our food comes from plants or animals. The amount of potential energy in food is measured in **calories**. Our bodies break down food to give us energy. Every second of every day, we use energy. Energy lets us grow, sleep, think, talk, run, and read. Like all living things, we need energy for everything we do.

Your body breaks down and digests food to get energy to live and grow.

We use a lot of energy when we run fast on a soccer field. The more we move, the more calories we burn!

Show What You Know

1. What is energy?

2. Why do your hands warm up when you hold a mug of hot cocoa?

3. How long does it take for coal to form?

Glossary

calories (KAL-uh-reez): the unit that measures the amount of energy in food

electricity (i-lek-TRISS-uh-tee): form of energy caused by movement of an electric current

fossil fuels (FOSS-uhl FYOO-uhls): fuels formed from the remains of plants and animals that lived hundreds of millions of years ago; coal, oil, and natural gas are fossil fuels

hydropower (HYE-druh-POW-er): electrical energy generated from running water

kinetic energy (ki-NET-ik EN-ur-jee): energy resulting from motion

photosynthesis (foh-toh-SIN-thuh-sis): the process by which plants make their own food using the Sun's energy

potential energy (puh-TEN-shuhl EN-ur-jee): the energy stored in something determined by its position or chemical structure

solar (SOH-lur): having to do with or coming from the Sun

Index

calories   20, 21

electricity   4, 15, 16, 17

fossil fuels   18, 20

hydropower   16, 17

kinetic energy   8, 14

motion energy   14, 15, 16

nonrenewable energy   18

potential energy   8, 9, 14, 18, 20

renewable   12

solar energy   12

temperature   11

wind   14, 15

Websites to Visit

www1.eere.energy.gov/kids/

www.eia.gov/KIDS/ENERGY.CFM?PAGE=4

http://climate.nasa.gov/kids/greenCareers/renewableEnergyScientist/

About the Author

Buffy Silverman writes science and nature books for children. She likes to use her energy hiking in the woods near her home.

Ask The Author!
www.rem4students.com